1000 Plot Twists for Your Next Novel

S L Lethe

© Copyright 2016 - All rights reserved.

In no way is it legal to duplicate, copy, or transmit any part of this document in either electronic means or in printed format. Recording of this publication is strictly prohibited and any storage of this document is not allowed unless with written permission from the publisher. All rights reserved.

The information provided herein is stated to be truthful and consistent, in that any liability, in terms of negligence or otherwise, by any usage or abuse of any policies, processes, or directions contained within is the solitary and utter responsibility of the recipient reader. Under no circumstances will any legal responsibility or blame be held against the publisher for any reparation, damages, or monetary loss due to the information herein, either directly or indirectly.

Please note the information contained within this document is for educational and entertainment purposes only. Every attempt has been made to provide accurate, up to date and reliable complete information. No warranties of any kind are expressed or implied. Readers acknowledge that the author is not engaging in the rendering of legal, financial, medical or professional advice.

TABLE OF CONTENTS

Introduction

Supernatural/Fantasy/Horror Based Plot Twists

Quest Based

Plot Twists for all Genres

Murder Mysteries

Objects/Artefacts

Romance

Conclusion

About The Author

Introduction

Writing a novel is harder than you may initially think. Anyone who tells you that it isn't is either lying or have never written one themselves. Even today, after writing over 250 books myself (fiction and non-fiction, from 10,000 to 100,000 words), I can still feel the pressure of coming up with a work that captivates and entertains the reader.

There are many ways to create a book your reader's will enjoy. Characters need to well-rounded and develop through the course of the book; you need to show, instead of merely tell what is happening; and readers want to be kept on the edge of their seats. For first-time writers, this can be daunting.

This is where *1000 Plot Twists for Your Next Novel* comes in. Plot twists help develop your story, keep things going and pushes the characters to grow. Your heroine may start off a timid little mouse but through several twists during the book, she ends up becoming a strong, arse-kicking woman who can take on the entire world by herself. Or your hero discovers through the love of one woman, he can be more than what he ever dreamed of.

The plot twists in this book are those I have collected, stored, and used myself over my years as a writer. Every writer will use these twists differently, stamping their own designs on them. Use them as much as you want and create a masterpiece of your own.

The plot twists are divided into several main categories for those who need help with certain genres.

Happy writing!

Supernatural/Fantasy/Horror Based Plot Twists

- You are a young vampire passionately in love with a mortal but your thirst for blood could kill them. You hear of a cure in a distant place, where a vampire can become human once again.
- You can command the forces of nature as you travel across a ravaged land whilst being hunted by monsters.
- An earthquake has devastated a beautiful, peaceful land, resulting in monsters roaming above ground once more as a wicked sorcerer makes his bid for ultimate power.
- You must close the doors/gates of the Underworld before dark spirits and demons ravage the land.
- You are bespelled by a vampire.
- Come face to face with your demon side.
- You are on a riverboat cruising down the Mississippi River when you come across a vampire carrying an ancient artefact which draws you to it inexplicably.
- You discover a vial of pure light which has the power to dissolve dark gates and doors.
- The only ones who possess the information you seek are the fairies who have been kidnapped. To

retrieve the information you need, you must first rescue them.
- You need to speak with Baba Yaga but the witch who can magically transport you to Russia can only send you so far.
- You are sucked into an enchanted painting.
- A fairy throws dust at you, now you can fly.
- A sorcerer sucks all the magic out of supernatural creatures.
- Your companion is thrown off a cliff and you must use what you have on hand to save them.
- You begin to have psychic visions.
- At midnight, the guests take off their masks at the ball. The faces are worse than the masks.
- You must rely on a goblin to get you out.
- Your healing skills are renowned throughout the kingdom and you are brought to a strange land to heal a young princess who cannot speak.
- A sequence of numbers turns out to be a magical formula.
- A witch turns your male main character into a girl briefly.
- A bear kidnaps the bride at her wedding.
- You see a child with glowing red eyes decapitating a bunny with a pair of scissors.
- You need to pass through a room or house full of demon-possessed children.
- Monsters swarm out from underneath the bridge you need to cross.
- The Tree of Life is dying and the seasons are getting mixed up.
- The door freezes over before your eyes.

- You are accused of dark magic, an accusation which can lead to the death penalty, in the middle of town by someone you hate.
- Due to political reasons in the magical community, the heroine has false memories implanted.
- Everything the old tales say turns out to be true. This turns out to be the worst thing for your characters.
- You are tasked with the job of escorting the souls of the dead to the Underworld. Only one of the souls is a past lover/former friend.
- Time is running out but the remaining time has been cut short. Now you are forced to seek help from someone you know isn't trustworthy.
- In order to progress, you must first speak with a family of monsters so fearsome they were only spoken of in whispers.
- Your sister begs you for help when her son begins to age before her eyes. You discover she has made a deal with an evil witch and your nephew is paying the price.
- A mass of fires has spread throughout the city and it is believed that it is the legendary phoenix which is to blame.
- An ordinary fishing village has been transformed into a nightmarish landscape as the recently buried have begun to rise from their graves.
- You've purchased a house only to discover it's haunted by restless spirits, and only you can see and hear them.

- In order to escape unconsciousness, you must realise that it's different to escaping a real location.
- You must gain the permission of the king to venture into a strange and dangerous land, but the king refuses to rule.
- Make the next scene all about ghosts – they start popping up all over town, frightening the people and causing chaos.
- A vampire has been keeping a slave town hidden for years and you need to get in there to rescue a blood slave.
- It is revealed that you are carrying another soul within you.
- Your spouse dies and their spirit tries to communicate with you, using your body. What are they telling you?
- To escape, you must keep your body still.
- You must cross a field of toxic flowers which are spreading out in all directions.
- An empath who can calm angry people around her.
- You use dragon's blood to heal someone but it creates a permanent blood bond between the two of you.
- You have been dreaming of a person for years, never believing they are real until one day you suddenly cross your path. You follow them, only to find yourself wrapped up in the supernatural world.
- It turns out vampires can walk during the day.
- A shifter discovers an antidote to repress the shifter gene.

- You are thirsty but the only water supply is a polluted river and all the animals nearby are dying from it.
- Allow yourself to be worshipped as a god/goddess.
- One of the nine muses come to inspire you to do great things, but it ends up going terribly wrong. What terrible beauty have you unleashed upon the world?
- You are helped across the water/sea/river by selkies, seals who can turn into humans when they shed their skins.
- Threaten to slit the throats of anyone who refuses to kneel to you.
- A 300-year-old beauty secret has effective yet deadly results.
- You perform a knowledge spell but it goes wrong and you start hearing voices.
- You open an ancient box only to let loose angry spirits and dark demons.
- Just as you start to be able to control one power, another one appears, only this one is far more destructive and chaotic than the first.
- The situation is made direr when a sea monster attacks.
- Your human roommate turns out to be a vampire.
- Information that you desperately need is given to you by an animal.
- You find yourself during a clan of vampires. Will you be their next meal, or their saviour?
- Your lover tells you they possess magical/supernatural powers. Do you believe them?

- To escape, you must go through the garden. What horrors will you find out there amidst the roses and vines?
- A vampire hunter masquerades as a rock star.
- To bind a demon, you must first interpret the positions of the stars.
- A swarm of bugs delays the next step.
- You awake from a dream but you don't know what is real and what isn't.
- You are at the theatre or a concert when a vampire/sorcerer bespells the entire audience, ordering them to capture you.
- In order to gain information, you must have a conversation with a spirit. Make a sacrifice at a local shrine.
- Meet a dryad when you start building a tree house for your young son.
- You need to answer a riddle by the Sphinx, but if you guess incorrectly she will eat you.
- An undine tempts a minor character to their watery grave.
- He's from ancient Greece and she's a modern-day New York gal.
- The magic only works on the Summer and Winter Solstice.
- You are transported from your bedroom into a castle by magic.
- A magical or man-made creature attacks you.
- Ghosts come to your rescue against vampires.
- You can only save yourself by using salt.
- A creature produces little stones every time they lie/get stressed.

- An exorcism doesn't go to plan. There is more than just a ghost in the room.
- You find that there are two different species of humans.
- You fall asleep by a stream only to be transformed into a mermaid!
- A spell causes everyone in the room to be romantic, apart from you.
- A wicked spell leaves you immortal.
- You follow a strange animal only to find yourself in a new world.
- You touch an object only to be transported to the land of the Elves.
- You discover your grandmother was a fairy who fell in love with a human.
- The room you are standing in suddenly transforms into a magical forest.
- You practice your musical instrument only to hear someone clapping when you're finished – but there's no one there!
- Seek out the witch at the crossroads and make a wish, only for her to refuse to grant it.
- Dig up a dead body to find the answer you seek.
- Reveal the hidden demon inside you – literally. What does the demon do to those in the same room as you?
- Head to the basement where you discover hundreds of jars containing body parts and unusual specimens.
- Those born under a certain constellation become powerful warriors with the ability to reshape the world.
- Survive a lethal injection.

- Change the nature of the vampire.
- You fight off a demi-god.
- Ghosts attack you.
- A banshee starts wailing outside your house. There are five of you inside. Who has she come for?
- Give birth, but not to a human child.
- A dryad seeks revenge when her sacred grove is cut down.
- A newspaper, dated to tomorrow, tells of your death.
- A couple on honeymoon drive themselves insane when they begin having nightmares.
- You go to the circus ... only to find it's a circus of the damned.
- You get a spooky message from beyond the grave through the television.
- A human is transformed into a vampire before your very eyes.
- The cure is worse than the supernatural disease.
- All the air is sucked out of the room you're in.
- An immortal wants to die but can't do it by themselves. They ask you to kill them.
- You lock the door and board the windows, but the vampire comes through the ceiling.
- A deceased loved one comes back to haunt you in this scene.
- Sign up for a ghost tour, only to discover ghosts are real.
- The Furies – the vengeful goddesses of Greek mythology – seek retribution on you for a past crime.

- You become ill only to discover it's the ability of someone bad.
- Combine death and water in one scene – the dead walk out of the ocean, your character dies in a swimming pool.
- Your sister is turned into a vampire and now you must try and decide whether you're going to behead her or not.
- Face the Triple Goddess – Maiden, Mother, Crone – and discover your fate.
- All the traditional ways of killing a vampire don't work!
- Set the next scene in a stationary vehicle; a creature destroys the car, a magician uses magic to trap you inside ...
- You interview a patient at a mental institution who claims that a ghost is haunting him.
- You discover your child has supernatural abilities when you walk in their room.
- You discover your baby/mother is a fairy changeling.
- A ghost watches a movie with you in a cinema.
- A child's imaginary friend causes real trouble.
- With a single word, you can create life.
- With one word, you cause someone to die, their ghost to remain Earth-bound for all eternity.
- All the wine in the house turns to water.
- Your fairy godmother is not a nice fairy godmother.
- You are forced into a greenhouse to seek shelter but it's full of carnivorous plants.
- You insult the Prince of Vampires ... only for him to fall in love with you.

- A warrior from 10th century Scotland is brought to life.
- You call forth a demon with hilarious results.
- A genie grants you one wish.
- Red Riding hood turns out to be a vampire.
- A trip to the museum results in you relieving a memory from your past life. The security guard thinks you're trying to steal a valuable object.
- Perform a séance.
- You discover you're being followed by a vampire.
- You are the only one who can tell when a vampire is close by.
- You don't recognise your friend now he's been transformed into a werewolf.
- Both the werewolves and vampires want you ... who will get to you first?
- Make the next scene an exhilarating fight scene between two supernatural creatures – a vampire against a gargoyle, a werewolf against a fairy.
- You still feel the presence of your deceased spouse in the house. Only it's not a comforting presence.
- A friend of yours admits they've joined a group that protests supernatural creatures, and you're a werewolf/fairy/vampire.
- A knight, who was transformed into a statue, returns to life.
- You come across a giant spider but it's friendly and likes to play games.
- A gargoyle comes to life and carries you away from danger.
- A vampire and werewolf fall in love.

- The vampire you fell in love with was the same one who killed your family.
- Magic – make the next scene all about magic. Cast a spell – does it go horribly wrong or does it create something positive?
- Something confronts you when you don't believe in magic.
- Pain, terrible physical pain. A vampire, a Fae warrior or a dwarf torture your character.
- True love's kiss awakens something deadly in you both.
- The death of someone transforms them into a hideous, bloodthirsty beast set on killing everything in sight.
- A superstition turns out to be true.
- Your boyfriend is killed before your eyes by a witch who drains the life out of him.
- She gains immortal beauty through the lives of others.
- You come across a beautiful woman bathing in something terrible; the blood of her victims, their entrails or a bubbling potion.
- Set the next scene in a dark crypt, only illuminated by candles.
- You witness the birth of a gargoyle.
- Your paranormal investigator friend calls on the phone but all you can hear is deranged laughter and their screams.
- Arriving home, you find it being torn apart by fairies. What are they searching for?
- Your horoscope tells you how you're going to die.

- A deranged dentist turns out to be the tooth fairy in disguise. They will have your teeth whether you like it or not.
- A witch informs you that you were born a witch and proves they are telling the truth.
- Your companion is possessed by a demon and tries to kill you.
- A shifter shifts in front of you with comical results.
- You're invited into a vampire's home but everything inside does something strange.
- You discover the tapestry the goddesses of Fate have weaved for you – only for you to take their scissors and hack it to bits.
- You are transported to Mount Olympus but you are not welcomed.
- You have the choice to become a vampire to save your brother. Do you embrace it or do you let your brother die?
- See a glimmer of decency in a bully/abusive person.
- A witch transforms you into a pig for an hour with hilarious consequences.
- A geeky high school student defeats the big, bad warrior.
- You receive a magical tattoo for protection.
- Spiders come out of everywhere! They pour out of holes in the walls, scuttle across the ceiling and from under the doors.
- The vampire you thought was scary turns out to be comedian.
- Lightning strikes you.

- Someone must willing sacrifice themselves on Samhain for the greater good.
- You're chasing a vampire when you come across one of his victims who now tries to bite you.
- You're scratched by a werewolf and must decide whether to kill yourself or not.
- A single word causes you incredible pain.
- You fall down a hole only to wake up in 200 CE in Roman Britain.
- The only place to rest for the night is at a motel full of strange, spooky characters.
- Make a wish ... and watch it come true right there and then!
- Your magical sword disappears when you wake up.
- You are sold to a wicked prince as his concubine.
- A curse which causes them to be ugly during the day but beautiful at night.
- You encounter a shifter in wolf form but don't realise who it really is.
- Your lover admits he's a shifter. When he transforms, it is not a ferocious creature as you were expecting.
- You save a were-lion who rescues you from your enemies.
- The vampire overlord agrees to let you go but only on one condition. You must face a deadly creature in the pit to win your freedom.
- While in werewolf form you are pinned down by humans and chained with silver. You must escape!
- A rumour goes around that you know the secrets to alchemy. There's a mob outside your door.

- You discover that every night all the women are locked in their rooms without exception.
- You look in the mirror and see something terrifying! When you look over your shoulder you discover there's nothing there.
- A god appears before you, forcing you on your knees.
- To escape, you must impersonate an ancient goddess.
- A goddess speaks to her people through your body.
- A Siren refuses to sing; her voice will lead to the death of her human lover but the urge to sing is strong.
- You must brew a potion to send the guards off to sleep, only you've never mastered this potion before.
- A flock of birds surround you as you are walking home.
- Due to a technology, your group finds themselves in hell.
- A magical bubble surrounds your town. You can't get out, supplies can't get in and everyone is going crazy.
- The Alpha of the local werewolf pack turns out to be your father.
- You learn that there is a prophecy going back thousands of years which tells of the destruction of mankind ... and the image of you is shown on the scroll.
- The vampire prince allows you to escape from his domain, but only if you return to be his bride in a month's time.

- You are offered a pill to wipe your memories of the supernatural world, or a potion that will turn you into magical creature.
- A cruel priestess turns out to be your mother.
- A vampire hunter mistakes you for a vampire.
- Due to an experiment by a warlock, your character can perform amazing fighting skills.
- A fairy-tale princess from a cursed book materialises before your eyes ... only she isn't all as sweet as the book makes her out to be.
- Others look to you to lead them when they rebel against their vampire overlords!
- The ruler of this strange, fantastical land knows who you are because they, too, are from Earth.
- An ancient pack law means your immediate execution.
- A mad alchemist proclaims themselves to be God – then angels appear.
- You end up in another time period due to a strange potion.
- An angel's wings are not as soft as they look.
- Beauty, torment, binding, and fire are strongly associated with this form of magic.
- A veil of mist appears before you – if you step inside, you won't know what's on the other side. Do you dare take the risk?
- Battle a god and win at a terrible cost.
- A magic spell turns you into a witch.
- Your car is run off the road by a witch chasing a werewolf. Then they spot you.
- Creatures are after you, but they can hide in direct daylight. Only the darkness can destroy them and you're petrified of the dark.

- A solar flare causes a character's life to change for the worse.
- Unexpected deaths/accidents come in threes.
- A Celtic warrior queen is reincarnated as you.
- A demon child stalks you.
- Evil spirits can't cross a line of salt but you can only find bath salts ...
- An owl brings a warning of death.
- Your daughter is the target of a vengeful ghost.
- He wants to touch you, but if you let him he will be cursed.
- Lilith, the Queen of Hell, offers you a tempting deal but is it worth it?
- You are offered a drink, but it is spiked with a magical potion.
- Step forward and you save yourself; step backwards and you save your partner. Where do you go from here?
- There is more than just gold waiting for you at the end of the rainbow.
- Sitting in the forest, you prepare to die. Who, or what, comes out to watch and play?
- A tiny fae creature transforms into human size. They tell you they want to kiss you.
- Practitioners of this form of magic are affected by the phases of the moon, and need to use silver and mirrors to do so.
- You fall into a mirror – only to discover another world on the other side.
- The Eight Immortals of Chinese Mythology kidnap you but do you really want to escape?

- You land into a giant spider's web. Can you escape before you are dinner?
- Bubbles – make the next scene all about bubbles. Make the oceans bubble, play in a bubble bath, blow bubbles with the kids …
- Each time you use this magic/magical object, you become sick. Too many times using it will result in your death.
- If you could change what you know is coming, would you?
- Someone calls your name, but when you get up no one is there.
- Cast a divinatory spell and discover something completely different.
- You're in a castle when you see the ghost of a long-dead queen running away from something, a look of horror on her face.
- In the dead of winter, it suddenly becomes hot enough to boil your skin off.
- Cerebos, the three-headed dog who guards the entrance to Hades, becomes your faithful companion.
- You can only use this magic at night.
- Every time you get too close to the demon it teleports you away.
- A fairy can grant your wish, but it doesn't turn out well for your loved ones.
- You discover you can harness the power of the sun, but only for a minute each day.
- An angel possesses the body of your child/lover to give you a warning.
- You visit a fortune teller to have your palm read. The tarot cards fly around your head, three

specific cards laid out perfectly before you. What do they tell you?
- The seer dies in front of your eyes, her body turning to ash/liquid which can be used.
- You need the mermaid's permission to cross the river. Only you jumped into the water before you ask.
- Only 16% of the population have survived a magical calamity.
- You, as a human, are fighting off a vampire when a giant ice spider emerges. How does this effect the fight?
- The secondary character is revealed to be a different species than what they originally believed, due to a long-hidden affair.
- The inhabitants of this land are descended from British/Roman/Mongolian settlers who escaped to find a safer place to live and still speak the original language.
- A semi-divine priestess rides upon a giant mechanical spider/scorpion.
- The blood of a strange creature turns into scorpions and spiders when it touches the ground.
- Pegasus, the divine winged horse from Greek mythology, swoops down to rescue you from Hades.
- You cannot access this magic without offering sacrifice.
- Accuse the character of being the double.
- A spell causes the evil side of your personality to come to life.

- Hades has decided to cast aside Persephone and wants you at his side despite you refusing his advances. Persephone agrees to the new match.
- Friday 13th is extremely unlucky for you.
- A water spirit lives their underwater liar for you even though it will kill them.
- Knock on wood. The wood answers you.
- Birthmarks on your skin indicate where you were stabbed/shot in a previous life.
- Run over a grave; a skeletal hand reaches up and grabs you by the ankle.
- While folding the laundry, a goblin jumps out at you.
- An incubus/succubus falls in love with a human priest/nun/priestess.
- You are tempted off the path by a korrigan, an elf-like creature ready to lead you to your doom.
- The White Rabbit from Alice in Wonderland is a gorgeous man who leads you to temptation.
- Go on a magical carpet ride.
- The Ten Plagues of Ancient Egypt make an appearance in your hometown.
- The hero needs an important substance, and it can only be found in the lair of a vampire/demon/shifter.
- Hades offers you a pomegranate.
- You are offered a place at a school of supernatural creatures. But you're human ... or are you?
- You can only learn this magic during the day/at night or at a location.
- An autopsy reveals the character was pregnant with a strange creature.

- The secondary hero turns out to be an artificial lifeform.
- The lamia of Greek mythology pays you a visit.
- You are the human descendant of the Mother of All Vampires. Guess who is coming for dinner?
- A monster chases you through a corn maze. Can you escape before they catch up with you?
- A monster brainwashes you.
- The plague returns, deadlier than ever!
- Act according to a silly superstition, only for it to save you/send you to your doom.
- Your magical abilities include decay, strength spells, conjuration and growth are considered its central attributes.
- Access to the gods allows you to use magic.
- Your exact double turns up at the same time, claiming to be the real you. Chaos commences.
- Carve a pumpkin only once the candle is it, it comes to life.
- You can control insects with your mind.
- To see the future, you must interpret the entrails of a sacred hawk at midnight.
- A companion falls into a pool of acid.
- A gigantic creature strikes fear into the hearts of the villagers, but just wants their love.
- Worship a goddess and be blessed in return, but the blessing causes havoc for those around you.
- These practitioners are widely distrusted in the magical community but you need their help. They want something in exchange for their aid.
- The vampires/fairies/werewolves are just getting ready for a 19-day celebration.

- Genetic coding turns out to be magic, not science.
- It is revealed, that to survive, the world depends on necromancy.
- A scientific experiment enhances magical abilities.
- A magical disaster reveals the truth of the matter.
- The vampire leader forces you to pick who will be food for the night and who is to be transformed into a creature of darkness.
- A fairy evolves into an angel before you.
- Use hypnotism to control your foes.
- A divinity protects your adversary.
- Death comes for you ... to take you out on a date.
- An angel falls into hell, becoming a demon, in front of you.
- Watch your friend in a magic mirror as they are reincarnated.

Quest Based

- Your uncle dies under mysterious circumstances, but not before he hides a strange and powerful artefact he instructs you to find.
- Your favourite amulet, which has been handed down from generation to generation, begins to glow. Research into these glowing runes brings you into contact with the Norse gods.
- You need to visit a small, undistinguished town but find that all the inhabitants start disappearing without a trace.
- You need to retrieve seven gems to an ancient amulet to use its magic.
- You've spent your entire life looking for a cure for your sister and you've finally tracked it down to a small English town, but the town holds a secret which is centred around the cure. You must unravel the secret otherwise your hope for a cure will be lost forever.
- You make a drunken bet with your friends to enter the haunted house. Once inside, you are trapped by an apparition and must figure a way to get out safely.
- You must free the souls a twisted artist painted into portraits in exchange for the souls of your loved ones.
- Your headquarters are destroyed, making the situation even more critical.
- You find yourself stuck in a magical prison but you hold no powers of your own.

- An ancient pact between Heaven, Hell and Earth has been broken and you are destined to mend it.
- You must discover an ancient Fae court banished to the deserts which holds the key to save your own people.
- Before you can carry on with your quest, you must save a temple from destruction and protect a sacred medallion.
- You need to find the sacred Medallion of Righteousness to save your family's temple.
- The Three Gems of Buddhism will lead you to the promised land.
- A dark shadow has plunged the land in darkness and you are sent on a quest by the king to save the realm.
- You are preparing to leave your abusive husband but just before you can leave, your daughter is kidnapped.
- The sequence of the characters birth maps out the direction.
- The Order sends you to retrieve two sacred scrolls which were stolen. Only now the vampires are after them, too.
- You must venture into the Land of the Dead to talk to the ruler of it.
- Wherever it is you are travelling to – a building, a kingdom, a dimension – it suddenly doesn't exist.
- Find yourself 1000 years into the future for 24 hours before being transported back to your own time.
- The next step in your quest is revealed to you in a dream. Only the dream gives you the wrong information.

- A map which leads you to Valhalla.
- Someone gets sucked into another dimension/portal and it's all because of you.
- You find the desired object in the kitchen, of all places.
- You are informed that you are the only one who can undertake this quest but to fulfil the prophecy, you must first be cursed.
- If you fulfil the quest, you will forever be cursed.
- A prophecy reveals that you are the villain.
- Make your way through the six Buddhist realms of reincarnation to escape.
- You were meant to be there at a certain time with the object but you weren't. Now you must deal with the consequences of failing at your quest.
- You are forced to take the longer way around.
- A tornado reveals a shortcut.
- You take the short cut, only to discover it takes you somewhere completely different.
- You must search for the legendary Fountain of Youth to save your father.
- You are caught trespassing on forbidden land.
- Someone you hate offers you much needed help.
- You have one day to prove your identity before you lose your inheritance.
- You arrive at your destination but she needs you to kill someone who's bothering her first.
- The map was recorded on a series of tattoos ... now you must find who they were tattooed on before you can set off on your journey.
- Lightning marks the place where you need to dig.

- An asteroid lands in front of you. You discover a substance on it that gives you supernatural abilities.
- You are transported from Earth to another world. Upon which, the first person tells you that there is an order of execution for anyone bearing the same name as you.
- You must return to Earth within a month before you are killed but you don't know how.
- You fall down a hole and discover a whole new world.
- The veil between the worlds is breached. You cross over, but something else comes through at the same time.
- You must save the kingdom from the curse, but the ruler tries to stop you.
- Learn about the true enchantment of the cursed object otherwise the evil sorcerer will be able to use it.
- You try to cross the border but you can't. How can you get past? What is stopping you?
- You need to obtain a golden apple but it's guarded by a fierce dragon.
- A stray footprint leads the way.
- The hero lands up in a virtual reality program due to a technical glitch.
- We discover that an entire kingdom depends on a crystal to survive, and it's the same one you have been sent to steal.
- You must return the golden sword to the rightful warrior, but you don't know who it belongs to. Everyone is claiming it is theirs.

- You must find the 25 people who have been blessed by angels before demons kill them.
- The answer lies in the stars.
- The portal is sealed shut. There's no way to escape.

Plot Twists for all Genres

- A burning building causes delays.
- You must rely on wisdom and cunning over physical strength to pass a heavily defended gate/door.
- Your next scene is full of fire – a bonfire that goes out of control, burning candles etc.
- Something you need is on a plane but it crashes before it can land.
- To get to your destination, you must first cross a chasm so deep and wide that it is known as the Abyss. No one knows how deep it is or what lurks within.
- Falling – whether it's falling through the window, off a cliff, through the ceiling, your character falls through something.
- To go down somewhere, you must step onto an old rickety platform that threatens to give way.
- A mother abandons her children for good reasons.
- Your mother announces you are emigrating.
- Defuse an explosive argument between friends.
- The one person who has information refuses to talk to your main character for unknown reasons.
- You have no idea who you are.
- Take a chance on someone evil.
- The bridge you need to cross collapses as soon as you step foot on it.

- Make the next scene all about snakes – you must find a special object in the middle of a nest of snakes, or have to cross a room filled with writhing snakes.
- Something tempts your character into giving in or doing something, but if they do, they risk losing everything. How do they fight against this overwhelming temptation?
- The infant son of your friend is kidnapped to draw you out of hiding.
- It's a special occasion tomorrow and you are far away from home. You must travel by train or coach to reach your destination but there are constant delays.
- Write a scene which tells of your troubled background. Your parents were junkies who neglected you, and were constantly bullied at school.
- The character owes money to everyone and before you can speak to them about what you need, you are interrupted by someone who wants their money back, by any means necessary.
- Someone important to you/the quest dismisses your opinion.
- Someone pranks you on April Fool's Day.
- You are given a beautiful present, but you soon discover it is the source of unimaginable pain and chaos.
- Rebel against the ruling order.
- Question someone's authority, only for it to pass to you.
- Let loose someone else's secrets by accident.

- Be shoved in the back of an unknown van and be driven off in complete darkness.
- Major natural disaster time – earthquake, floor, tornado, snow blizzard. Make your characters' face Mother Nature in all her terrible beauty.
- An envelope full of money is pushed through your door.
- It is revealed that one of your characters had an unexpected child, one that they had adopted after their birth.
- Bring down the house – literally. Destroy an entire building.
- You think your champagne has been spiked.
- Build up one person's self-esteem only for them to destroy yours in return.
- You must help a runaway teenage bride and soon-to-be mother.
- You receive an invitation to a party which you are forced to attend, even though you don't want to.
- Whilst travelling, have an embarrassing accident.
- The character is revealed to have come from a parallel world.
- It is revealed that everyone is from a parallel world and it stems from an illegal drug.
- The only person who agrees with you is someone you hate. To progress, you must work together.
- A violent ex-boyfriend comes back onto the scene.
- A stranger steps in and tries to protect you but dies in the attempt.
- You are forced to return home to retrieve something but you start recalling dark, depressing memories.

- The main character is revealed to have a dangerous compulsion.
- You need to discuss information with the other person but they don't speak English, or not very well.
- Make the next scene all about water – a flood, a surging river or drowning.
- You need help from an ancient society of assassins.
- Your main character suffers a crisis of faith when faced with a hard situation – how does this affect them?
- A minor character is resolute in their faith in opposition to the main character. How does this affect the story?
- Come across a drunk character.
- Your main character is mistaken for someone famous, infamous or someone who did them wrong years ago, resulting in a crazy situation.
- Someone you don't expect knocks on your door.
- Your main character is in a museum or art gallery. An object sets off powerful memories of something significant to their character.
- A rumour divides your main character from her friends, family, and allies.
- Your only hope is a crooked politician.
- You choose an important decision on a coin toss.
- The person you admire and respect the most suddenly reveal themselves to be a bad person. How does your character cope with this new information?
- There is a name or place that no one mentions. But your main character does, resulting in trouble.

- Someone from your past arrives on the scene, determined to gain revenge.
- You must travel in an unusual way to arrive at your next destination, such as a hot air balloon or a bicycle.
- Your villain starts displaying unusual behaviour. Their second-in-command organises a mutiny.
- Just as you need to speed up, your characters get caught up in a celebration or festival, resulting in delays.
- Your character must face their worst fears. If they don't, they are going to lose everything they dream of.
- You're given 24 hours to put on a grand event.
- A quote from your childhood stops you from doing something wicked.
- Take advantage of someone's bad memories, even though guilt consumes you.
- Just when you thought you can relax, the ceiling caves in.
- Your character must invent a story to avoid being killed.
- At the worse time, a minor character falls in love with the worse kind of person for them.
- An innocent man is arrested after helping/saving you.
- Your main character risks it all to save someone they don't know.
- Stranded – make your next scene all about surviving somewhere your character doesn't feel comfortable. Maybe they've broken down in the forest in the middle of a snow blizzard, or kicked out of the car in the middle of a lonely highway.

- Hide in the trash!
- You are injected with a strange substance by the one person who claims to love you.
- Discover someone else has been impersonating you.
- Your mode of transport breaks down and there's nothing around you that you can use instead.
- The main character learns the organization he's working for is on the wrong side.
- You are forced to learn martial arts, but you are extremely bad at it.
- You must do something immoral, otherwise you can't save the person you love or rescue the damsel in distress.
- Your daughter accidently destroys something important/sentimental to you.
- Your words cause someone to commit suicide.
- A rude message on the answerphone leads to an awkward conversation.
- You are mugged at gun-point.
- Control the situation with earth/water/fire/air.
- Party time! Make the next scene at a fancy nightclub or a bar.
- You are forced to fight a stranger.
- Fail a drug's test.
- Move to a new house. Maybe your place burnt down or the landlord evicted you, it's time to move on.
- Overhear your family putting you down.
- You're going to be an aunt/grandparent/godparent!

- Judgement – your character is forced to be judged or to judge someone else.
- A job interview where you constantly say the wrong thing. Do you get the job or have you ruined your chances completely?
- Pride before a fall; give your character something to be proud off, such as a great achievement, before taking it all away from them.
- Girl time! A light-hearted and funny scene where girls go crazy of make-up, music and boys.
- One character teaches the other how to do something; a father could teach his son how to build a model aeroplane, a mother teaching her son how to fish now his father's dead.
- You catch a businessman being abusive to a young employee.
- You are responsible for looking after a young child; fostering, adopting, babysitting, with hilarious results.
- You take revenge on your abusive boss.
- You betray the trust of the villain's maid/servant.
- You find yourself walking in the most dangerous neighbourhood in town.
- You discover photos of yourself ... on your own phone.
- Go to the circus.
- Find yourself locked within a room.
- You find your little sister bullying a classmate.
- The hero ensnares the daughter of the villain.
- Dream. Where does your dream take you? What does it tell you?

- Lose the baby your character is carrying; miscarry a baby you didn't know you were pregnant with or discover the baby has died in vitro.
- Let go of all your anger which then infuriates your companions.
- Give into weakness and find a pool of strength instead.
- A fraternity/sorority hazing goes too far.
- Trigger a trap!
- Time to heat things up – write a sizzling sex scene.
- Make your character drunk. What kind of shenanigans do they get up to? Do they confess a secret or do they want to go jumping into the ocean?
- You are told not to do something by your boss but you do it anyway. Now you're in trouble.
- Your mother causes a scene in public.
- Ice, ice, baby; set the next scene in any icy environment. Maybe your characters go ice skating or a father takes his son on the ice fishing trip they've never had time to go on before.
- Lose the most important artefact in a large crowd.
- A teenager overhears her parents planning in leaving her/him.
- You discover a conspiracy.
- Something complicated gets proven to be simple in the end.
- Your face freezes into place unexpectedly.
- Describe your best qualities to an interviewer.
- Play a silly game with a friend only to discover something amazing.

- Try to purchase an object which isn't for sale.
- You discover that you were adopted when you were 10 months old.
- You tell the truth but no one believes you.
- A political crisis is caused by your mistake.
- Become sicker throughout the scene until you collapse.
- Get away with a crime.
- Your child is born with a deformity.
- Someone tries to recruit you into their strange organization.
- Take a leap of faith – literally. Jump from a high building, or jump from a moving car.
- Someone you care about insults you, but they see it as a compliment.
- You give up on something and it makes you depressed.
- You try your best at something, but it wasn't good enough and there are consequences to failure.
- He refuses to stop.
- React to the weather.
- You discover a stash of money in your partner's drawers.
- Your annoying younger sister turns up on the scene and deliberately upstages you.
- A friend rings you – you've made the news!
- You call a friend at 3am.
- Reveal an imaginative/creative side, which screws up other people's plans.
- Become suspicious of someone you have always trusted before.

- A sudden discovery reveals that a minor character is not who they appear to be.
- A naked man turns up on your doorstep!
- The secondary central character believes their life has changed for the worse - this turns out to be this is due to a miscommunication.
- Your date used to be in a relationship with the policeman/woman in charge of your case, and they despise you/your spouse.
- Discover a secret room/chamber.
- You must rig a competition – is it in your favour or someone else's?
- Your friend asks you for an honest opinion but hates the answer.
- You are determined to find the underlying cause of what he's been keeping secret but the information hurts you deeply.
- Hide on the ledge of your building to escape someone after you.
- Pretend to be someone else.
- Your friends are shot in front of your eyes, by a stun gun/tranquiliser gun.
- You tell your boss he's a disgusting excuse for a human being in front of everyone at work.
- Have a revealing conversation around a campfire.
- You need to use a big tool to get inside/outside – a blowtorch, a power saw etc.
- You are disgusted by a secret exposed to you.
- A character discovers they have a child they never knew about.
- You need the right paperwork but it's gone!
- You don't have the money you desperately need.

- Escape through the ventilation shafts.
- There is an obvious way to disarm the trap, but it is fake.
- Become involved in a legal dispute with someone you thought was your friend. Now your friends are choosing sides.
- You are offered the money you need, but it comes at a humiliating and terrible price.
- A pop star's/actor's identity is stolen and they need the help of a shop assistant to reclaim it.
- Sadness should be the main theme of the next scene – receive some terrible news, have something devastating happen to you, so your characters are filled with emotion.
- You encounter racism at work or in your family when you are expecting a bi-racial child.
- Your character suddenly becomes scared of your hero due to inhaling a strange substance.
- An incompetent character proves their worth in front of hundreds of people.
- Describe an early childhood memory.
- A colleague frustrates you when they've not done what they should have done and now it's going to affect you.
- A jealous best friend tears you down.
- Don't give up. Push through something terrible because you need to succeed.
- Have a funny encounter with a new friend.
- Be extremely impersonal towards the other character.
- Addiction – have your character attempt to break free of something they are addicted to. It could be

drugs, alcohol, coffee, tea, someone they are obsessed with, but have them struggle with it.
- Deny what it is right before their eyes.
- Everything is revealed to be an hallucination.
- Shatter your character's dream.
- Hide from your annoying boss by going under the desk.
- Search for a long-lost friend.
- Your parents go missing and now you need to inform the police.
- A character seems unreliable after you discover how vain they are.
- Have your extrovert become suddenly shy and cause them to panic in a new situation.
- An abortion brings back painful memories.
- Be nostalgic and have your character tell others about a childhood trip they enjoyed.
- A stereotypical character proves they are completely different to what was expected of them.
- A minor character must face their phobia head on before the hero can continue.
- A minor character cheers the main character up when they are feeling sad.
- Go clothes shopping, something your character hates, and end up filthy.
- A nerdy high school student proves to be tougher than the football jock.
- When you are finally alone, you do something weird or silly ... only to find someone is watching you.
- Enjoy yourself at a party but watch that enjoyment unravel at the end of the night.

- You refuse to go into work, or you quite your job.
- A riot causes necessary delays.
- You are blackmailed into committing arson.
- The ugliest person reveals themselves to be beautiful inside.
- Bring the magic of Mother Nature to life – have a scene where you are entranced by hundreds of fireflies flying through the night air.
- You watch as the driver in the car next to you blares up the music and convinces you to sing along with them in traffic.
- Everything is revealed to be as it should be, despite evidence to the contrary.
- Due to a fall, a character is disfigured.
- You're at the State Fair or a carnival when you bump into a group of people you don't like.
- You get hit by a baseball at a game.
- You're woken up at midnight by someone you despise.
- You get a letter through the post from your birth mother, wanting to meet you.
- You hate the holidays, now explain why they bring you so much pain.
- Meet up with a strange, eccentric family member.
- You discover you are suffering from late-stage cancer.
- You gain what you need but only by singing.
- Break a mysterious code.
- A chemical experiment goes wrong, killing thousands in one day.
- Be affected by a book so much that you start crying.

- The school bully starts chasing you.
- Dye your hair a new colour or get a new haircut and make people notice you.
- A lightning storm reveals someone's mental health issues.
- Your sweet heroine is forced to let loose her mean streak to survive.
- All your good plans fall apart with heart-breaking results.
- Kill someone if you haven't done so yet. Do it in a way that screams pain and heartbreak for the main character.
- More than one person is needed to disarm/trigger the trap for it to work.
- A seagull swoops down and steals your phone. Now how are you going to call for help?
- You are implicated in an abduction case.
- Money falls from the sky to create chaos.
- A mysterious package arrives at your house.
- Evoke a sense of coldness. Set the scene in icy terrain, a snow blizzard; but make the characters as cold as they can get.
- You and two others are hiding but they are caught. Now you have to save them but can you?
- Set the next scene inside a hardware store.
- Attempt a cover up and fail.
- You come across a dark room where two men are being held hostage. They convince you to free them.
- It's safer in the darkness than in the light.
- A cowboy/lawyer/actor convinces you to dance with them.

- You scold a young boy, who turns out to be the Duke's son.
- Reveal an inner demon.
- An angry customer causes disruption at work.
- Finish something you started a long time ago then do something with it ... destroy it, give it away.
- Your younger sister gets the news that there is a liver waiting for her at the hospital. Time to get her there.
- Kill off a beloved pet. Maybe the next-door neighbour's cat got hold of Pat the Rat, or the family dog must be put to sleep.
- Your shy character must give an intense and important presentation in front of hundreds of people. Her job depends on it, but someone else is watching her in the crowd.
- A character is revealed not to be as blood-thirsty as first imagined, which complicates things.
- You must lose all your money on purpose, but you're not allowed to give it away.
- A character lies, but the intention behind it is not how it seems.
- You suddenly start to hate another character, due to an irrational belief.
- Humour hides a world of pain. Can you heal it?
- You're having a conversation with a loved one or friend, but they keep repeating the same thing repeatedly.
- You have nothing to wear so someone gives you some clothes to wear but they are hideous.
- Wrap some gifts but then discover you've wrapped the wrong ones!
- Break a mirror. Is it seven years bad luck?

- Speak to a good friend about a bad situation but they only fixate on their shortcomings and circumstances.
- Wake up thirsty and grab a drink, only to discover something mind-blowing.
- Find £100,000 in cash on the way back from the school run.
- Go to a nudists beach.
- You find a baby abandoned behind a trash can.
- Ride in a hot air balloon.
- A rainstorm leads a character to reveal a sadistic side to their personality, creating difficulties for the others.
- An explosion knocks you off your feet.
- Go stargazing and tell of fantastical stories behind each of the constellations.
- You cannot win without losing something big.
- A mentally ill relative is wiser than you.
- Get caught in your own trap!
- We discover, due to personal reflections, that a character is a hallucination.
- You discover that everyone is addicted to an illegal substance.
- Make the next scene all about blackmail. A minor character blackmails your protagonist into giving them what they want, or your secondary hero blackmails a prominent politician with devastating results for everyone involved.
- Make a choice before your past catches up with you.
- Learn the secrets of your past before it destroys you.

- A riot reveals an irrational fear.
- Prepare for a religious event but you aren't happy with it.
- Honey gets you out of a sticky situation.

Murder Mysteries

- Uncle James was murdered two weeks ago under mysterious circumstances. Slowly, other members of the family are being poisoned and you set out to find the truth, only to find Uncle James faked his own death.
- The police have arrested the person they believe is responsible for several deaths but new murders have taken them by surprise.
- A man murdered was found to be having an affair with a beautiful dancer but vowed to put an end to it, just before he was murdered.
- You get a phone-call from the police saying that your adopted brother has disappeared after vowing revenge on the family.
- The answer lies in the story of Hansel and Gretel.
- Your parents died 20 years ago and their bodies have only just been found.
- You discover a mass grave of skeletons.
- Your investigator is suddenly poisoned.
- You discover the murder weapon in a child's toybox.
- To gain your next clue, you must look in a history book.
- Your main character must remain hidden in a painful position to hear vital clues or information.
- Steal or destroy the evidence.
- The alternative protagonist turns out to be the minor antagonist's father.

- The killer belongs to the Golden Dawn secret society who don't want to tell you anything in case he comes back.
- You must interrupt a funeral where you are given valuable insights from a grieving family member.
- Plants cause the murders.
- Kill off a minor character to speed up the investigation.
- Resurrect a minor character in some way.
- Someone is trying to kill your lover but why? The answer lies in a wronged lover.
- The serial killer who's been terrorising the town suddenly attacks you.
- An investigation of a killer leads to you leaving the country.
- You are forced underground to escape being arrested for a crime.
- You were arrested for a crime and break out of jail/prison using a mirror/spoon/needle.
- The serial killer holds an entire house hostage.
- You have studied serial killer's, or one killer, your entire life and now the police ask you for help.
- The stepmother suffers a mental breakdown and tries to kill her beloved stepchildren.
- Find the next clue in water.
- A dying confession clears up a mystery.
- The wardrobe hides more than just clothes. What secrets lurks at the darkest corners?
- Your father discovers the last piece of the puzzle but only gives it to you if you promise to go on a date with a girl he's picked out for you.

- You must engage the services of a criminal to catch the killer.
- You discover your partner has done something terrible – he's killed the suspect, attacked the witness, or stolen the mob's money.
- The killer and the police officer kiss each other.
- They said it was suicide but you find proof that it was murder.
- The killer murders your sister in front of your eyes.
- A psychic screams they know who the killer is, but no one believes them.
- A cold case is resurrected when a new murder looks as though the same unknown suspect did it.
- The next clue can be found in a flower pot.
- You must let someone else die to solve the case.
- You stumble over the half-hidden body of a murdered child.
- Someone pulls a gun on you!
- You let the killer get away!
- A dead body is found in a hotel with blood smeared all over the walls, but the body has no wounds.
- Your nephew is killed because he was the rightful heir to a large fortune.
- You fake your own death to escape from a terrible life.
- A rich man kills a poor boy by accident but shows no remorse for the act.
- The only witness to the murder is a young child who refuses to talk.

- A person gets on an elevator but when it opens next, they are dead.
- Learn a terrible secret – your parents finally admit that you had a twin but they were murdered.
- Someone confesses to a murder they didn't commit.
- You interview a patient at a mental institution who claims they have evidence about a murder but no one believes them. Do you?
- Your arrogant and obnoxious minor character shows their vulnerable side.
- In this next scene, make it all about one sense – touch, taste, appearance etc.
- Discover a clue in their Google history files.
- Playing by the rules gets you into trouble.
- A letter tells you when the next murder is going to take place … in five minutes.
- The king goes missing, along with his mistress, but there's blood in both bedchambers.
- The murder weapon is placed in your belongings but no one believes you didn't commit the crime.
- The evidence suggests it was murder, not suicide.
- The murder weapon was something strange or silly, an unusual object to use to kill someone with.
- You sneak into the murderer's lair only to hear them slow-clap at you in the darkness as they lock you in.
- You had the murderer but he got away.
- The killer taunts you.
- Kill someone using a plastic bag, but not by placing it over their heads.

- The murderer wants you to kill them.
- You want to kill the suspect but you are stopped.
- A child gets in the path between you and the killer but you fire your gun.
- You stop the killer with a tea cup.
- The murderer is in the same building as you. Where are they?
- The court loses vital information or throws it out.
- A national television station plays a video of you shooting the wrong suspect or an innocent bystander.
- The killer keeps ringing you at your home.
- The killer takes you hostage and tortures you but stops before you die.
- The geek stops the murderer instead of the police officer.
- Fireworks mask the sound of gun fire.
- You must run away from the masked murderer through the sprinklers.
- To gain information you require, you must give the informant something strange and unusual.
- The killer sets off a smoke bomb to get away.
- You suffer second degree burns when jumping through flames to get out of the killer's burning house.
- The victim is killed in humiliating circumstances.
- The killer is you.
- Someone betrays you.
- The killer is hunting victims according to horoscopes. Yours is next.

- The killer knows better than anyone else, but their lack of attention to detail will be their downfall in this scene.
- The police beat the hero/heroine.
- There's no motive for the killer to do what they do, they just like to mess with people.
- She wants revenge on the friends who didn't appreciate what she brought to the group.
- Your villain's incapability to deceive may turn out to be a fatal flaw.
- Your daughter's pony is slaughtered as a warning.
- The real villain is revealed and it's not who you thought it would be.
- The victim cannot be saved in time.
- The antagonist turns out to be the secondary hero's aunt.
- The police arrive but the only one who shows up is an ineffective, donut-munching desk jockey who doesn't take notes.
- A reversal of circumstances; someone who's rich becomes poor, or vice versa.
- Flip the switch; the subplot collides with the main plot. You are having trouble with your own relationship but your sister's new lover attempts to seduce you when they have a fight.
- Introduce a new enemy into the mix.
- The murderer's wife gives you valuable information.
- Kill a major character, one that you would never think of killing.
- Because of the murder, a character reveals their greedy side.

- The murderer is striking victims according to a children's nursery.
- The henchman is the key to solving the mystery.
- Your boyfriend is the killer. They murdered people to save/protect you and now they torture someone, forcing you to watch as they do it.

Objects/Artefacts

- An artefact capable of breathing life into something already dead.
- You are looking for something but you come across a multitude of dolls with no heads and dismembered teddy bears.
- The crystal skull of Morpheus, the god of dreams, was stolen.
- A magical amulet which requires seven small gems to complete – with each new gem, the amulet changes colour.
- You discover a castle which can talk, but it's sarcastic and likes it when people get hurt.
- You come across an artefact no bigger than your hand but it has the power to destroy an entire kingdom.
- An ancient grimoire that could lead to the destruction of everything.
- You discover that a mundane object given to you years ago turns out to be an important message.
- A book that makes you instantly smarter.
- A chair that forces the person sitting in it to tell the truth. Do you dare sit down?
- A cursed object that can only be cleansed with salt water – sea water or tears.
- The tool your character was using suddenly breaks. What do they do now?
- The discovery of an old letter reveals horrific information regarding the main character's family history, changing their plans completely.

- A necklace which curses whoever wears it.
- A knife that looks dull and rusty, but echoes with the screams of those that were killed by it.
- A deck of tarot cards which can speak the fortune.
- An earring that holds a drop from the Fountain of Youth.
- You pick up an amulet, only to find it contains a ghost.
- An embarrassing love letter is revealed – what consequences will there be?
- You find an old photograph of your grandfather but in a negative light – an old Nazi uniform perhaps?
- A small box contains a message inside but if you break it, the message will be destroyed.
- You discover a bow and arrow which could kill an immortal/god.
- A sword that sings.
- A music box which fills the room with such sad music they want to deafen themselves.
- A statue comes to life!
- You go through the belongings of your deceased aunt only to find something disturbing.
- The grandfather clock starts running backgrounds.
- The kitchen appliances start going crazy.
- An empty swing is swinging by itself.
- In every photograph in the house, a strange man appears, no matter where or when it was taken.
- You find the least expected thing in your father's desk drawer.

- A sarcophagus holds the physical body of a goddess.
- A nature goddess is trapped within a tree.
- A ring of toadstools marks the spot where you must dig.
- An ancient statue of a Greek god causes whoever holds it to become angry.
- An iPhone which tells the future, but only within an hour timeframe.
- A freezer holds a bloody surprise.
- At the bottom of a jewellery box you find a letter your mother wrote when she was younger apologising to herself.
- A child's plain wooden car can transform into a fast, magical vehicle on request.
- The bear-skin rug can hold conversations with you.
- An old boot is the Horn of Plenty.
- The All-Seeing Eye looks just like a marble and is hiding within a child's marble bag.
- The Diadem of the Queen of Heaven sparkles with the radiance of the sun but burns mortal flesh.
- A clock that when strikes, someone dies.
- A cloak of invisibility.
- The water in your shower suddenly turns blood-red.
- The lock will only open when you sing to it, but it only likes certain songs.
- While fishing, you pull up a strange bottle containing weird-looking smoke.
- A book which describes past or future events.

- 12 bronze statues of Shaolin Monks housed at a Chinese temple.
- A book which can suck you into the pages and force you to interact with the characters.
- A potion mixed with the blood of the wisest creature/person on the planet.
- A ring with the ability to show the way to a place of safety.
- An old slingshot saves the day.
- Six keys, all of which look similar, holds the answers but guess the wrong key and all is lost.
- A bird's nest hides a shiny and mysterious object which holds ancient secrets.
- A plain old shopping bag which can carry much more than initially thought.
- Twin bracelets that don't allow the wearers to move more than 15 feet away from each other before they can't breathe.
- A bowl of apples stands before you. Five are normal, two will change your appearance and one is poisonous.
- Paper cranes swarm around you, causing more bloodshed than a sword or axe.
- A cage which can only be opened by a bone.
- Go apple picking and discover a golden apple. A goddess will grant your deepest desire, but it comes at a price.
- Roses which bloom only with fresh blood.
- Your ancestral lands hold the grave of an ancient warrior. Inside the grave is a treasure box with their legendary weapons; weapons which can change your family's future forever.

- You find yourself duped into collaborating with an evil mass murderer to save someone you care about.
- A spice rack contains everything you need to succeed.
- A potion is introduced. It is used but it's use is far darker than what anyone could imagine.
- The next clue can be found in the coffee pot.
- The villain is the good guy and wants to save the world.
- The murderer reveals how the victim wronged them. The police officer agrees with them. Will they be allowed to escape?
- She is hurting others in her mission for martyrdom.
- See a penny, pick it up, all day long, you'll have good luck. Pick up an unusually shiny penny and enjoy great things for that day.
- The Golden Fleece of Greek mythology looks a lot like the old sheepskin rug that lays on the floor of your grandmother's house.
- An enchanted piano/band which plays by itself.
- An app on your phone which tells you how to kill someone.
- A medieval book bound in leather and written in blood.
- A handbook for identifying and executing supernatural creatures.
- A magical sword is destroyed at the end of the fight.
- A house where the floors map out all directions.
- A mysterious suitcase is introduced but is never opened, even at the end.

- You need to make an important potion but it's made from dangerous creatures.
- A religious text is analyzed and everything is not as it seems.
- A vibrant painting of a wizard reveals the truth about where you came from.
- Open an old weathered chest only to be blinded by what's inside.

Romance

- Your main characters are enemies. Perhaps he's purchased land to build a fancy golf resort and she wants to turn it into a butterfly sanctuary, or he is a real estate developer and she's a small business struggling to stay afloat.
- Your main character has never dated before – perhaps due to religious reasons, or a family situation – and doesn't know what to do when someone indicates they are interested in her.
- He's cheated on her in the past. After so many years apart, he wants another chance but the pain of his infidelities makes her wary.
- Bring out flaws of both characters at the same time. Maybe one is too negative, the other too stubborn.
- The mistress destroys the brother/sister of her lover.
- She's not interested in dating anyone who she considers beneath her.
- Both characters are competing for the same project at work or for a client.
- Back in the past, they were lovers but she betrayed him. However, he finds out that there was a good yet unexpected reason for the betrayal.
- Your main characters were dating but then one gets a promotion which should have been the other's.
- Fall in love with someone who is gay.

- Discover a secret rendezvous between your father and someone you don't know, and confront him.
- A previous affair comes back to haunt you.
- Develop a crush on someone who is already married and tell them how you feel.
- She hurt his family, damaging their reputation. Was it intentional or just an accident?
- Your spouse is hit on by a beautiful young woman right in front of you.
- Your female character was abused by her ex-husband and now has trust issues.
- A long time ago, your character was hurt badly and a relationship now can threaten to expose that pain.
- Your character meets someone incredible but due to bad choices in the past, she's hesitant to take the next step.
- You agree to go on a date with someone your best friend fancies and they find out.
- Your character meets someone amazing but find it hard to trust you. How are you going to convince them that you are worth the chance?
- Your characters meet for dinner but the waitress is their ex-girlfriend.
- You discover your partner of six months has two children from an old marriage they haven't told you about.
- Make your next scene all about pets – you take Rover out for a walk only for them to chase a stranger's dog, someone's dog jumps all over you, or perhaps a kind stranger saves Fido from drowning.
- A test will bring you closer.

- In the past, she's done something so terrible that she feels that she is just not worthy of love. How does this news affect her lover?
- Your male character finds himself in love with his sister's best friend.
- You just start dating when you find your sister is in love with him, too!
- Out on a romantic date, everything is going beautifully, when your partner's ex-wife starts arguing with him.
- Two good friends find themselves wanting to take things further, but one is hesitant in case it ruins the friendship.
- You go to the bathroom only to discover a freaky secret ...
- You discover your rich boyfriend is a con man.
- The sister secretly dates the mistress.
- You run across an old friend who tells you that your girlfriend was in prison for a serious crime.
- The characters are from different social circles – he's an aristocrat and she's the baker's daughter – and these differences are highlighted when meeting friends or family.
- Your relationship was meant to be a secret ... until your horrible brother tells everyone, resulting in someone getting hurt.
- A group of you are in an accident and he saves someone else instead of you.
- The next scene should feature cars – go for an exhilarating car ride, cruise along the coast, go to an old car exhibition – and discover what cars mean to your character.

- Your character was faking interest in the other person – maybe they are a reporter going undercover – until they fall head over heels for them.
- By accident, you find out that your lover made a bet with their friends whether they could get you into bed.
- He's a bad boy but you're sick of being a good girl.
- You were rivals initially but the need to work together has developed into something more. Only you don't want to admit it.
- Your abusive partner wants another chance, even though you had him arrested.
- You want him badly, but he's hesitant because you're his best friend's sister.
- Your character falls in love with someone emotionally damaged – they've buried a child or has suffered a terrible experience.
- Your different religions are meant to keep you apart. Does it?
- You introduce your new partner to your family only they don't like them and are extremely vocal. How does your character act when they continually put him/her down?
- It's time to take things to the next level, only you find they are into bondage or something else. Whatever it is, your character does not want to be a part of it.
- A clash of cultures – your stuffy Asian in-laws meets your hippy American parents, or your Indian family meets your weed-smoking friends. Either way, bring on the clash of cultures.

- Returning home from your date, you find your fiancée's wife standing on the doorstep.
- Can it ever be? Your characters are in love but he tells her he's marrying someone else.
- He makes a move on his long-term crush ... but she wants someone else.
- They start dating but she wants someone else in addition to him. Can she decide about who she wants or will the decision be made for her?
- She refuses to give up her other lover.
- You make big romantic plans but she tells you she is going away. Maybe she's going abroad to study, or she's dying, but either way, she's not going to be there.
- Are you going to make the ultimate sacrifice for your partner? Whether it is the dream job, the perfect house, you must decide as to what is more important.
- They tell you they want to try for a baby. Only you're not ready.
- Years ago, doctors explained she could never have kids and she never told him. Now he wants to try and she must decide whether to confess or not.
- A few too many drinks led to a drunken one-night stand with the one person they shouldn't – a rival, someone you hate, or your partner's sibling?
- At first, his appearance frightens you, but slowly you find yourself drawn to them.
- The police show up at your door to arrest your partner.
- She has kids from a previous relationship and this makes you hesitant.

- Their reputation – a womaniser, abusive drunk, ex-drug addict – causes you to stop and think whether you should be getting involved or not.
- You decide you cannot move to another country with your husband/wife.
- An awful start; a small car crash involving their extremely expensive Porsche, or fighting over the last car space.
- Something pisses your character off and they take it out on their partner.
- Your love has been involved in a terrible accident. Will your boss let you leave work to go to them, or will they refuse to let you go?
- She tells him she loves him but she needs her freedom.
- He loves her but he loves his job and doesn't want distractions.
- It was only meant to be casual sex but things are starting to get deeper. But only on one side.
- No sex allowed! Your character is meant to abstain – due to religion, culture, or their job – but the temptation is extremely powerful.
- Your lover tries to kill you – tells you they were sent to kill you but they can't do it.
- Your assassin lover is forced to kill you.
- Your character is starting to get far too bossy for her liking and she puts her foot down. No one tells her what she can and can't do!
- She hits your mother or father.
- You see your boyfriend hit a woman.
- You discover your father abused your mother throughout their marriage and now you can't trust any man ever again.

- Your lover suddenly disappears!
- Someone offers you money to sleep with them and you don't have enough to pay the rent.
- Your lover is kidnapped by bank robbers and now you must rescue them.
- Just as things are heating up between the two characters, someone interrupts them – their child, parents, boss ... either way, they can't carry on with what they want to it.
- The job gets in the way; maybe you're working overtime to pay the bills but she wants to spend time with you.
- Drugs – the next scene should be all about drugs. You discover your boyfriend has been selling drugs to pay for your medical bills, or that they've stolen the pills your father needs to live.
- An obsessed fan causes shocking consequences when you're out on a date.
- You throw up on the person you secretly have a crush on.
- Kiss a stranger. Whether it's a stranger, someone you fancy or part of a drunken bet, pucker up those lips!
- A wedding that causes both happiness and sadness at the event.
- Your boss fires you when you refuse their affections.
- Your stepbrother confesses he has loved you for years ... even though you're married.
- Your family are shocked when you confess that you are gay.
- You tell your boss, who makes a move on you, that you are married to his son.

- You discover your boss is the woman you fell in love with years ago, but who spurned you.
- You steal money from your parents to elope but discover he has left the country without you.
- You follow your wife to an unknown location when you suspect her of having an affair.
- Two men propose to you at the same time!
- Your fiancée's father kisses you, and you kiss him back! Who walks in on you at the same time?
- You catch your boyfriend stealing money from you so he can run away with his mistress.
- Your boyfriend catches you in bed with your lover. The outcome is quite enjoyable.
- You discover your feelings for someone only after they sleep with your colleague.
- Your affair is discovered and made public.
- You discover your boyfriend convinced your sister's lover into breaking up with her.
- You answer an ad looking for love.
- On your honeymoon, you find you are one of several women he has married.
- You agree to marry him, but only for business reasons.
- Write a sex scene but make it funny.
- He resigns from his job so he can date his colleague.
- She refuses a date from a colleague.
- Bring your character out of their shell; perhaps she's the shy and quiet around friends but when things are heating up between the two of them, she's wild and uncontrollable.
- Receive or give a romantic gift.

- The truth gets the girl.
- You meet someone from an online dating website, only they turn out to be different from their profile picture.
- You finally leave someone but still love them.
- Girl talk – you discuss previous boyfriends and can't believe what you saw in them.
- She loves you but you confuse her.
- Even though you've been together for a year, your lover's parents try to set him up with someone else.
- Your spouse loses their job.
- You lose your job just when they lose theirs. How will you survive?
- The best man at your wedding reveals an embarrassing secret.
- Your spouse finds you're in serious debts.
- Arrange a date at somewhere you hate ...
- Humiliation causes you to run into your dream man.
- A dream man turns out to be a complete nightmare, and the nightmare man turns out to be the real thing.
- You bring your date home, but you hate the condition of your home. Especially since they live somewhere far grander.
- Your in-laws pressure their child into divorcing you.
- You fall in love with the geek.
- Someone disgusting tries to make a move on you.
- You just want sex and the only person there is the one you can't stand.

- Sacrifice – make the next scene all about sacrifice. Maybe you discover your spouse sacrificing his pride to give you what you want, or you sacrifice a treasured object to pay for rent.
- You meet your star crush who asks you out.
- A fan tries to seduce you.
- Love conquers all. Even in the most despairing situations, true love can conquer anything.
- Have your main character describe true love to a minor character.
- A new love looks the perfect likeness to your ex-husband.
- Describe a dream of something your character wants to achieve and let it inspire the other.
- Break your character's heart so that it will never be pieced back together properly again.
- You give up on your love because they don't care about you anymore.
- A pet causes an argument between lovers.
- An argument between minor characters causes a rift between the main characters.
- Get your female character to describe their dream date, only for their lover to do the complete opposite.
- A waterfall reveals the beauty within.
- Go skinny dipping with hilarious yet sweet results.
- Sleep outside under the stars with your lover.
- Your enemy refuses to return something important to you unless you marry their daughter/sister.
- True love's kiss won't save you; it will condemn you all.

- A battle between two enemies for the love of one girl. Who will be victorious on this battlefield?
- He wants to touch her but she's afraid of him.
- The bad boy does something exceptionally sweet for you, but grumbles whilst doing so.
- He's made a bet with the guys to seduce him ... but she secretly knows about it already and is playing him along for her own bet.
- Your son introduces his new girlfriend ... only to introduce a single mother of five kids and covered in tattoos.
- She gives him one night to change her mind. He's determined to make every second count.
- He wants more than what she can give.
- After so many years of being alone, how can you be in relationship now?
- She trusts him with her heart, but not with her body.
- Your male character comes on too strong.
- He does something exciting for you, but can you depend on him?
- Coax your lover out of his comfort zone. Take him to the ballet, do something crazy, make him feel a whole new man.
- She wants to commit to you but finds it hard to discuss things. So, she gets drunk to try and loosen up but ends up in the back of a police car.
- Your wedding dress is ripped to shreds by the cat.
- Your girlfriend is still mad at you for hurting her feelings earlier so won't help you when you request something from her now.
- A breakup reveals a new talent.

- He treats you like a princess but tries to run the house like he's the king.
- She nags you continually when you get home until you snap. How far did you go?
- In death do you depart; a minor couple dies together instead of one living without the other.
- His secretive nature drives you crazy.
- She asks for something different in the bedroom.
- You fall in love with a voice and seek it out.
- Discover your sweet, innocent girlfriend is a famous erotica writer.
- Your mistress tells you she is getting married and your fiancée tells you she is pregnant.
- To complete their destiny, your main character must kill their true love ... and they can't bring themselves to do it.
- An accidental kiss by the adversary creates complications.
- The antagonist suddenly develops an obsession with the hero's sister/aunt/friend.
- A mistress finally leaves her lover ...for his wife/son.
- You must kill someone you love, and you do it.
- The protagonist discovers that his family are plotting against him.
- The heroine falls in love with the secondary villain.
- Contempt becomes infatuation.
- Politics divide lovers.
- Your boyfriend becomes jealous of an old flame or current friend.

- Comfort a friend who's just been dumped by her lover.

Conclusion

I hope you have found these plot twists of great use. It can be hard to plot out an entire book beforehand, and it can be just as hard for writers who just write as they go along. Sometimes there will be occasions when you get so far into writing your book that you just don't know where to go; you essentially write yourself into a corner and you don't know where to go from there.

A great plot twist can turn things around instantly, taking you and the reader, into a completely new direction. Plot twists can make the reader gasp and grasp the arms of their seats, compelling them to keep reading. It can also help you, as the writer, figure out where you want to go with the story.

And with that, I wish you all the best in your writing career!

About the Author

S L Lethe is a full-time author, writing more than 250 books under various names, in a wide range of genres. She lives in the UK with her children, books, and dreams.

Printed in Great Britain
by Amazon